By A Heart That Will Always Remember

A LOVE

THAT WAS NEVER

MINE

—— Mohit Singh

"Some loves are born knowing they will never be returned,

yet they love anyway—silently, endlessly, without reason or reward.

To carry a love that has no home,

to hold on when the world says let go—

that is the ache of loving someone who was never yours,

and yet, will always be."

DISCLAIMER

This book is a deeply personal reflection of unspoken love, longing, and loss. While inspired by real emotions and experiences, it remains a work of personal expression rather than an exact recounting of events. Any resemblance to actual people, places, or circumstances is purely coincidental.

The words within these pages are not meant to cast blame, assign guilt, or rewrite the past—they are simply an attempt to give voice to emotions that were never spoken aloud. This book does not seek closure but serves as a space to honor a love that was never mine.

Readers should approach this with an open heart, understanding that love, even when unreciprocated, can be as real and profound as any love that was returned.

Table of Contents

INTRODUCTION

Some love stories end in togetherness, while others, like mine, remain suspended between dreams and reality—where love is deeply felt but never fully realized.

This is not just a love story; it is a journey of holding on and letting go, of hoping for a future that only ever existed in my heart.

I loved her—not with the kind of love that flickers and fades, but with a quiet, unwavering devotion, the kind that remains through lifetimes.

It wasn't a love that demanded or pleaded; it was simply there, constant as the stars that burned in the night sky—distant, unreachable, yet always present, even when hidden behind clouds.

She was my beginning, the moment my world shifted, the force that turned the ordinary into something extraordinary.

She was my end, the place where all roads led, the last thought before sleep, the ache that refused to leave my soul. She was the whispered prayer I never spoke aloud, the silent wish I sent into the universe, hoping somehow, some way, it would bring her back to me.

And yet, she was never mine.

Not in the way I longed for, not in the way love stories promise.

She was the dream I woke up from too soon, the unfinished melody that played endlessly in my heart.

She walked beside me, laughed with me, shared transient moments that felt like forever—but forever was never ours to have.

Still, if given the choice, I would love her all over again. Even knowing how it ends. Even knowing that some hearts are destined to beat in the same rhythm but never in the same embrace.

Through letters never sent and poetry left unfinished, I write to her—the one who became my world, the love that shaped me, the dream I will always carry. This is not just a story. It is a collection of moments, of memories too precious to fade, of emotions too heavy to keep locked away.

If love is meant to be shared, then let these words be my offering, my confession, my farewell.

I write not to seek closure but to preserve what once was—to honor the love that, even in its incompleteness, was the most real thing I ever knew.

I write because there are things I never had the chance to say, truths I was too afraid to voice, and feelings that refused to die even when the person they belonged to walked away.

This is for the girl who never truly belonged to me but still became the most important chapter of my life.

This is for the nights spent wishing, the days spent pretending, and the endless moments caught between hope and heartbreak. This is for the love that was never mine, but in some ways, will always be.

Because in a world of endless choices, I had only one: her. And without her, there is no one else. No second option, no alternative love story waiting to unfold. Just her. Always her.

There is an ache in carrying a love that has no home, a longing that never finds its resting place. It is like holding onto a star that has already burned out—its light still reaching you, even though it no longer exists.

I wake with it, sleep with it, and live each day knowing that no matter how much time passes, this love will remain suspended in the spaces between what was and what will never be.

And yet, I do not regret a single moment of it. I do not regret the way my heart chose her, how it made a home in her laughter, how it memorized the rhythm of her presence like a song played on repeat. I do not regret the stolen glances, the quiet conversations, the way she made the world feel softer just by existing in it.

To love her was to experience something infinite, something that surpassed time, logic, and reality itself. It was a love that defied endings, that refused to fade even when she walked away. It was the kind of love that didn't need to be returned to be real.

Because it was real—it breathed within me, shaped my days, and filled my nights with both warmth and sorrow.

And even now, even in the absence of her touch, her voice, her presence—I carry it still. Not as a burden, but as a part of me. Because some loves do not disappear. Perhaps we were never meant to have our story unfold here, in this version of reality, but in another—where timing is kinder, where choices don't pull us apart, where love doesn't have to be left behind.

And so, I will continue to carry her within me. In the whispers left upon my lips,

In laughter lost, yet still persists.

In silent beats my heart still keeps,

She dwells untouched, where time won't reach.

Through letters never sent and poetry left unfinished, through dreams that slip through my fingers like sand, I will hold on—not to the hope of changing the past, but to the certainty that love like this cannot simply vanish.

So, I wait.

Not here, not now, but beyond the reach of this lifetime.

Until the day our paths cross again, in another time, in another life—where love finally gets to stay.

I loved you in the quiet spaces,
In the pauses between my thoughts,
In the spaces between heartbeats
Where your name was always caught.

I loved you in the way the moon
Still waits for the sun to rise,
In the way the ocean longs for the shore,
In the way hope never truly dies.

I found you in forgotten melodies,
In the scent of rain on restless streets,
In the words I never spoke aloud,
In the dreams I lost but still repeat.

You were my almost, my could-have-been,
The story written in fading ink,
A love that burned like dying embers,
A ship that sailed but couldn't sink.

And though the world has moved beyond us,
And though you're now a name untold,
The love I gave still hums so softly,
Like a song the winds will always hold.

The Beginning

A Message That Changed Everything

Loving you was never a choice; it was an inevitability, a force as natural as breathing. From the moment our worlds collided, I knew my heart had found its home in you. And yet, in all the ways that mattered, you were always just beyond my reach—like a beautiful dream that vanishes the moment I wake.

It all began with a message—a simple exchange, a small connection.

When I discovered that our pasts had unknowingly intertwined long before we met, it felt like a sign, a thread tying us together in ways we had yet to understand. That common ground became the starting point of something that grew slowly, quietly, like a seed taking root in my heart.

At first, it was just conversation. Then it was offering small kindnesses, being there in ways that felt effortless yet significant. And somewhere along the way, I found myself falling—falling in a way that I couldn't stop, even when I knew there was no ground beneath me. What mattered was our bond, the space we carved for each other in a world that never promised us a future.

So, I told you.

I let my heart speak, knowing well that it would not change things. But I did not tell you with the hope of rewriting fate. I told you because my love was never about claiming you; it was about cherishing you. And so, despite everything, I stayed—not because I expected anything in return, but because I wanted to. Because having you in my life, in whatever form, was better than never having known you at all. You were not just a person to me; you were an entire world, a constellation of all the things I admired and longed for.

I fell for you in the way your mind worked—how it felt so familiar, so in sync with mine. We saw the world through the same lens, our thoughts mirroring each other's, as if our minds were two halves of the same equation.

There were moments when I would start a sentence, and you would finish it with the exact words I was about to say. We reacted the same way to life—laughing at the same jokes, sharing the same frustrations, finding solace in the same quiet moments.

It felt as if I had found my reflection in you—only a little softer, a little more impulsive, a little more unpredictable, but in all the ways that mattered, the best.

I had always been drawn to intelligence, to ambition, to people who carried dreams as heavy as their hearts.

And you were both—a dreamer with a fire inside you, someone who wanted to carve out her own place in the world. I saw that passion in your eyes, in the way you spoke about your future, in the way you refused to settle for anything less than what you deserved.

You weren't just beautiful in the way the world defines beauty—your eyes, your smile, the way your hair framed your face—you were beautiful in the way you existed. In the way you carried kindness like an unspoken promise. In the way you gave without expecting, in the way you saw the best in people, even when they didn't deserve it.

You were beautiful because of the strength you didn't even realize you had. You were, without a doubt, the most extraordinary person I had ever known.

Every moment spent with you felt like something rare, something I wanted to preserve in a place where time could never reach it. The late-night conversations, the silent understanding between us, the way we could sit together and not say a word yet still hear everything. It was as if we spoke a language that belonged only to us—one that didn't need words to exist.

I remember the first time I realized just how much you meant to me.

It wasn't in some grand, cinematic moment. It was in the little things—the way you gently played with your hair while lost in thought, the way your face lit up when you talked about something you loved, the way you always knew exactly what to say when I was drowning in my own mind. It was in the way you made even the simplest moments feel significant.

But love, as I learned, does not always come wrapped in the gift of forever. Some love stories are written in the margins of a book that will never be finished, in the quiet spaces between heartbeats.

Ours was one of those stories—beautiful, momentary, and impossibly real.

I carried you with me in ways I didn't even understand at the time. I would find you in songs I had never heard before but somehow felt like they belonged to us. I would see you in places we never went to together, but that I wished we had.

I would hear your voice in my head, giving me advice you never actually spoke, but that I knew you would have said.

You became a part of me, woven into my existence, a ghost of something both beautiful and unfinished.

And even now, after everything, I know this much is true—I was never the same after you.

Maybe I never will be.

You came like a whisper, soft and true,
A fleeting spark, a sky so blue.
I never chose to love, yet still, I fell,
Into a story only time could tell.

You were a fire I could never hold,
A dream too vast, a tale untold.
The stars aligned, then pulled apart,
Yet you remained, etched in my heart.

I loved you not to claim or keep,
But in the silence, vast and deep.
In moments brief, in stolen time,
In words unspoken—never mine.

You walk a path where I can't be,
Yet still, you live inside of me.
Not as regret, nor as pain,
But as a love that still remains.

If not this life, then let it be,
A love beyond eternity.

A Love That Felt Real

As we talked, I slowly realized that you belonged to someone else. You never mentioned it at first, and in a world distanced by silence and screens, there was no way for me to know. But deep inside, I had always sensed it.

There was something about the way you hesitated before speaking, the way you left certain things unsaid. And yet, even as my heart braced itself for the truth, I never wanted to ask.

Some part of me knew that once the words were spoken, there would be no unknowing.

Then, one day, you finally told me. You confessed your fear—that if I knew, I would leave. But I wasn't like that. The fact that someone else had already claimed the title of yours didn't change what I felt for you. It didn't alter the way I looked at you, how your presence alone could quiet the storm inside me.

It was never about possession, never about erasing the life you had outside of me.

It was our bond that mattered to me, and I wanted to make it stronger. So, I promised you I would stay—no matter where life took us. And I did—without expectations, without demands, without asking for anything in return.

Then, life resumed. Distance faded. And for the first time, I stood in front of you—not through the glow of a screen, not as a voice carried over a call, but as something tangible, something real.

It was a cold winter night, the air crisp with the scent of fading autumn. I still remember the way your hair swayed gently in the wind, how the glow of the streetlights reflected in your eyes. But more than that, I remember the weight you carried, the unspoken pain behind your usual brightness. I had known you long enough to read your silence, to understand the burdens hidden behind your small smiles.

So, I asked. And instead of replying, you hugged me. Then, you broke down. Your body trembled in my arms, and I felt the warmth of your tears against my shoulder. I didn't speak. I just held you.

In that moment, I wished I could take away all your pain, that I could make things right. Then, between broken sobs, you told me you didn't want to be with him anymore. You needed a way out. And though every selfish part of me wanted to believe it was because of me, I knew that wasn't the reason.

You had your own struggles, your own reasons.

And as always, I helped you—selflessly, without thinking of my own heart. I even told you to reconsider, to be sure of what you wanted. I wanted you to be happy, even if it wasn't with me. But despite my words, despite the rationality I tried to uphold, a quiet hope took root in my heart. Maybe now, I had a chance.

So, I tried. I gave you all of me, put in every effort. And you noticed it. We grew closer. We spent hours talking—day and night, sharing thoughts, fears, and dreams. We held hands. And when you hugged me, it felt like home.

I still remember the way I kissed your forehead and whispered, I will always be here for you.

We were happy, in ways I had never been before. You never said you loved me, but I saw it in your eyes. The way you looked at me—it was something deeper than words, something even love couldn't define.

You became my safe place, and I became yours. We traveled home together, shared secrets, and trusted each other completely.

You never said you loved me. Not in words, not in confessions whispered in the dark. But I saw it—*oh, I saw it*—in your eyes.

In the way they softened when you looked at me, in the way they searched for mine across crowded spaces, as if the world only made sense when our eyes met. In the way they flickered with a thousand unsaid words, in moments where silence carried more weight than any conversation we ever had.

I saw it in the way you laughed—how you would turn your head just slightly before you did, as if you were shy about letting me see that side of you. In the way you held back your smile for a second too long, as if deciding whether or not to let yourself feel the happiness I gave you.

And when you did smile—God, it felt like the world paused for a moment.

I saw it in the little things. The way you would lean in when I spoke, as if my voice was the only one that mattered. The way you always noticed the smallest changes about me—when I cut my hair, when I wore something new, when my mood was off even if I swore I was fine. The way you held on just a little tighter when we hugged, as if you wished you could stay in that moment forever.

You never said you loved me. But I saw it in the way you let your guard down around me, in the way you could be your truest, most unfiltered self. How you shared your fears, your insecurities, the stories you had never told anyone else. The way you looked at me like I was something special, like I was someone who truly mattered.

I saw it in the way you hesitated. In the way you would start to say something but stop yourself, as if afraid that once spoken, the truth would change everything. In the way you searched for reasons to be close, to sit beside me, to hold my hand, but always pulled away before it could mean something more.

You never said you loved me.

But I saw it in your eyes.

And sometimes, I wonder if you saw it in mine too.

For the first time, it felt like we were in love—with each other. And in that moment, nothing else mattered. But love, no matter how deep, cannot always withstand the weight of reality. There were walls I could not cross, pieces of your heart that still belonged elsewhere. I told myself that love was enough, that my presence was enough.

But slowly, cracks began to appear. You pulled away in moments I least expected, you hesitated when I reached for you. And yet, I held on, because how could I let go of something that felt so real?

But fate is cruel.

And love, unspoken, is sometimes never truly known.

I held you close but never tight,
For love is free, not bound by might.
In silent glances, in fleeting touch,
I saw my world, I saw too much.

You never spoke, yet I could hear,
The words unuttered, crystal clear.
A love unclaimed, yet deeply known,
A fire that burned, though never shown.

I watched you drift, I let you be,
For love is not a lock, but a key.
Yet in the dark, when no one knew,
My heart still whispered back to you.

Perhaps in time, in lives anew,
I'll find my way, I'll reach to you.
And in that world, where fate is kind,
You'll be my love, and I'll be thine.

But in this life, I'll Walk alone,
With love unclaimed, but never gone.
For though we part, and though you stray,
I'll love you still, beyond today.

Beyond tomorrow, beyond regret,
A love not lost, but not quite met.

Not in this world, not in this time,
But in the next—you will be mine.

The Night, The Stars Fell Silent

Everything was going exactly as I had wished.

For the first time, the world felt like it had aligned with my dreams, as if fate itself had conspired to bring me closer to her. I had built a life around the moments we shared, no matter how brief. I held onto every small sign, every glance, every unspoken word.

I convinced myself that even if she never said it out loud, I could see it in her eyes—the same love that I carried for her. But life has a cruel way of reminding us that dreams are just that—fragile illusions, held together by nothing more than desperate hope.

And for me, it all fell apart in a single night.

A night that took everything away, leaving me with nothing but regret and emptiness.

One night, everything shifted. What should have been a moment between us became something else entirely. The voices of others grew louder than our own, drowning out what could have been understood. And in the end, the world decided our fate before we even had the chance to.

A mistake. One that I would regret for the rest of my life. It wasn't something irreparable. It wasn't something that should have destroyed us. In another world, in another story, it would have been a misunderstanding—one that could have been fixed with an honest conversation, with trust, with time. But we didn't live in that world.

We lived in one where people lurked in the shadows, waiting for a moment of weakness.

Waiting for a chance to twist the truth, to poison the air with their interference.

People always need a reason to break in, to play the hero in their own eyes, even if it means destroying something sacred. Those I had once trusted, the people I called friends, betrayed me in the worst way.

They took what should have been a private moment between us and turned it into something ugly, something larger than life. They took my words and twisted them, took my actions and distorted them.

I was left helpless in the chaos, standing alone in a storm I had no power to calm.

And worst of all, I couldn't find her. Not really. I searched for her eyes—the eyes that once held warmth, trust, and love. But when I found them, they were different. Clouded. Uncertain.

She wouldn't even look at me.

I tried to speak, tried to tell her to listen to me just once. But I was already drowning in the noise of others—voices feeding her doubts, whispering fears into her heart.

I wanted to scream, to make her understand that what was happening wasn't right.

But it was too late. She had always cared about what people would say. Their opinions mattered to her, dictated her choices. And me? I never cared about the world, not when it came to her.

I would have fought for her, defied everything for her. But that was where our difference broke me.

I would have chosen her over everything. But she let the world come between us. And then came the final blow. The one that shattered whatever was left of me.

A guy she called a friend saw the gap that had formed between us and walked right in. A friend? No, a true friend wouldn't have done what he did. A true friend would have tried to fix things, to help us find our way back to each other. But he saw an opportunity and took it. And just four days later, I saw her—the girl who had once spoken to me every moment of the day, the one who had once found solace in my presence—laughing with him. Smiling. Telling people how she had spent the whole night talking to him instead.

I stood there, shattered beyond repair.

Any sane person would have walked away then, let anger take over, let resentment replace love.

But I couldn't.

Even in that moment, even after everything, I still loved her.

I still wanted her.

I still held onto the hope that maybe, just maybe, she would turn back. That she would see through the lies, that she would remember what we had.

But she never did.

I watched her slip away, and all I could do was stand there, watching the world I built around her collapse.

She was gone.

The night was cold, the winds stood still,
As silence wrapped the air so chill.
The stars above refused to shine,
For they too knew, you weren't mine.

A whisper lost, a word unsaid,
A love once bright, now cold and dead.
I reached for you, you turned away,
A story ended in dismay.

The echoes rang of all we were,
Yet in your eyes, I saw the blur.
Of distant dreams and fading light,
Of love that lost the will to fight.

And though the world had won this game,
My heart still burned in endless flame.
For love like mine does not decay,
It clings to time, though you walk away.

I wonder if the stars still shine,
In skies where you are no longer mine.
Or do they, too, weep in despair,
For love that vanished into air?

If fate had willed a kinder end,
Would you have stayed, more than a friend?
Would you have fought the world for me,
Or was I always meant to be free?

Yet freedom tastes of hollow pain,
Of longing nights, of love in vain.
And though you live in tales untold,
My heart still burns, my hands stay cold.

For I was yours, in light, in shade,
In love that time could not evade.
Yet here I stand, alone, undone,
A love that lived, yet came to none.

Numbing the Pain

Chasing the Ghost

After the incident, we tried to ignore each other, but it's never that easy. How do you turn away from someone who was your entire world just days ago? Our eyes still searched for each other in the crowd, pretending as if everything was normal. But nothing was. She was still trapped in the thoughts of those who had taken her side, worried about what they would think.

She sacrificed me for people who, one day, would move on with their lives, leaving her behind as just another passing memory. But I understood—this was who she was. It was never about me.

I was used to talking to her every day. Her absence left an unbearable silence. Sitting idle for even a minute became a torment, each empty second filled with thoughts of her. I tried everything—going home, distractions, forcing myself to move on. But nothing worked. The memories didn't fade; they only grew louder in the quiet.

So, I turned to something I never thought I would. I drowned myself in alcohol, cigarettes, marijuana—anything that could blur the edges of my pain. I lived in a haze, always stoned, always drunk, always out of my senses. It didn't make me forget her; it just made me think a little less. And the less I thought, the more I wanted to stay numb.

At first, it was just a drink—just one, just to take the edge off. Just to dull the weight pressing against my ribs, just to silence the voices that whispered her name in the quiet spaces of my mind.

The first time the burn of alcohol hit my throat, I coughed, wincing at the unfamiliar sting. It tasted terrible, but the warmth that followed, the slow, deceptive comfort it offered—it was enough. For a few moments, the ache inside me dulled, the sharp edges of my heartbreak softened, and I felt… lighter. Not happy, not whole, but at least I wasn't drowning in her memory.

But one drink wasn't enough.

Because the moment it faded, the pain came rushing back, stronger, heavier, suffocating. So, I took another. Then another. And soon, I wasn't drinking just to forget—I was drinking because I didn't know how to exist without her.

Cigarettes followed. I never liked them before. I used to hate the smell, used to wonder how people could be addicted to something so destructive. But the first time I inhaled, I understood.

It was not just about the nicotine—it was about having something to hold, something to fill the emptiness in my hands where her fingers used to be. It was about watching the smoke curl into the air and pretending I could send my memories with it, letting them disappear into nothingness. I'd sit there, cigarette in hand, watching the embers burn down, wishing I could burn away my feelings just as easily.

And then came the weed.

I was never the kind of guy who needed an escape. I always prided myself on my control, my discipline, my ability to handle anything life threw at me. But heartbreak wasn't something I was built for. Losing her wasn't something I could just "handle."

It was a wound that refused to close, an ache that made breathing feel like a chore. *So, when someone offered me a joint one night, I did not even hesitate. I took it, inhaled, let the heaviness settle into my limbs, let my mind detach from reality. And for the first time in weeks, I wasn't consumed by thoughts of her.*

But the thing about numbness is that it's addictive.

It wasn't long before I was chasing that feeling every single day. Morning, afternoon, night—it didn't matter. I needed to stay high, stay drunk, stay far away from my own thoughts. I stopped caring about classes. Stopped caring about my future. The guy who once had dreams, who once stayed up late talking about ambitions and plans, had become a ghost of himself. I wandered through the days in a haze, my mind fogged, my heart buried under layers of artificial oblivion.

People started noticing.

At first, they tried to talk to me, tried to ask if I was okay. But what could I say? That I was drowning? That I had become someone even I didn't recognize?

I laughed it off, told them I was just *"having fun," just "living a little."* And they believed me—because it's easier to believe someone is okay than to acknowledge that they're falling apart right in front of you.

Day and night, I filled the air around me with something stronger than my grief, but no matter how much I tried to fade the memories, they never truly left. Because the truth is, you can drown your body in alcohol, suffocate your lungs in smoke, flood your system with chemicals—but you can't erase love. You can't drink away the way she made you feel. You can't smoke out the sound of her laughter, or the way she looked at you when she thought you weren't watching.

Nights were the worst.

During the day, I could pretend. I could wear a mask, force a laugh, throw myself into meaningless conversations, and convince the world—maybe even myself—that I was fine. I could distract myself with noise, with people, with anything that kept me from facing the emptiness inside me. But the moment the sun set, and the world quieted down, when the distractions faded, and I was left alone in my room with nothing but my thoughts—I lost. Every single time, I lost.

The ghosts of our memories crept in like unwelcome visitors, whispering everything I wanted to forget but never could. They came in fragments, flashes of moments so vivid they felt more real than reality itself. The way she used to hold my hand, the way her fingers curled around mine so naturally, like they belonged there. The way she rested her head on my shoulder, sighing softly, like she had finally found peace in a chaotic world. The way she looked at me when she thought I wasn't watching eyes filled with something unspoken, something I swore felt like love. I replayed it all, over and over, like a film stuck on an endless loop. No matter how much I tried to shake them off, the memories refused to let go. They clung to me like a second skin, an inescapable weight pressing down on my chest, making it hard to breathe.

I would lie in bed, staring at the ceiling, tracing the cracks as if they held the answers I was searching for.

But they didn't. Nothing did. Sleep became a distant, unreachable thing. Some nights, I lay awake until the first light of dawn crept through my window, my body exhausted but my mind relentless. Other nights, I would give in to my vices—drowning myself in alcohol, lighting one cigarette after another, hoping the smoke would fill the void she left behind. But nothing worked.

I wanted to reach out. God, I wanted to call her, to text her, to find some excuse—any excuse—to hear her voice, to pretend that we could still be something, even if it was just a fraction of what we used to be. My fingers hovered over my phone too many times, typing messages I would never send.

Do you miss me? Do you ever think about me? Are you happy without me? But I knew the answers. She had moved on. While I was still here, stuck in a past that no longer existed, sinking deeper into my own destruction.

I stopped recognizing myself.

I would catch glimpses of my reflection in windows, in bathroom mirrors, in the dark screen of my phone, and I wouldn't know the person staring back at me. His eyes were hollow, lifeless. His shoulders slumped as if carrying a weight far too heavy to bear. The boy who once smiled so easily, who found joy in the simplest things, was gone.

All that remained was a ghost of him—a stranger who didn't care anymore, who didn't feel anything except the constant, gnawing ache of loss.

And in that haze, I learned something about people.

The same voices that had once screamed against me, the same faces that had cast their judgment without hesitation, now sat beside me as if nothing had ever happened. *They drank with me, laughed with me, and pretended the past was nothing more than a misunderstanding—an insignificant mistake that could be erased with time.* The ones who had stood against me, who had whispered behind my back, who had fueled the fire that destroyed everything I loved, now leaned in close, offering empty apologies between sips of their drinks.

"Maybe we were wrong," they said.

"Maybe we judged too soon."

Maybe?

It was almost laughable—how effortlessly they shifted, how easily they forgot the weight of their own words. They spoke as if their apologies could rewrite history, as if their regret could somehow undo the damage they had done.

But what was the point of their sorry when the only person that truly mattered was no longer in my life?

They had already taken everything from me. Their accusations, their interference, their self-righteousness—it had cost me her. And now, here they were, trying to wash away their guilt with liquor, as if that would be enough. I watched them, listened to them, but I felt nothing.

No anger, no satisfaction, no sense of justice. Just emptiness. The same people who had once torn me down now acted like my closest friends, as if they had never been on the other side. It made me realize how quickly people switch sides, how easily they change their allegiance when it suits them. Loyalty, convictions, even so-called friendships—they were all just illusions, fragile and transient.

And yet, despite it all, I had won.

I had outlived their judgment, survived their betrayal. The same people who had tried to break me now sought my company, treating me like one of their own. I had proven them wrong, forced them to acknowledge their mistake.

But at what cost?

I had lost the only thing that truly mattered.

I had lost her.

I burned the nights with smoke and gin
Yet still, her name lived deep within.
A ghost that danced in every flame,
A whisper soft, yet still the same.

I filled my lungs with bitter air,
To chase a love no longer there.
But memories don't drown in wine
Nor fade with every borrowed high.

The glass ran empty, yet she stayed,
A phantom love that wouldn't fade.
No matter how much I would drink,
She stained each thought, each breath, each blink.

I drowned in crowds, yet felt alone,
In empty touch, in hearts unknown.
I chased the high, I blurred the pain,
But every road still spoke her name.

I let the smoke curl through my chest,
Hoping it'd quiet my unrest.
But every exhale spelled her name,
And every drag still burned the same.

I begged the stars to let me go,
To take the weight I couldn't show.
But even when the dawn would rise,
Her shadow stayed in my eyes.

No drink could drown, no smoke erase,
A love that time could not replace.
And though I fell, and though I bled,
She lived in every tear I shed.

I burned the nights, I cursed the past,
But love like this was built to last.
No fire could scorch, no storm could quell,
A love that hurts yet loves too well.

The Hollow Days

Where Time Moves, But I Remain

There comes a point when even pain stops feeling real. It no longer claws at your chest with the sharpness of fresh wounds, no longer sends you doubling over with grief so raw it leaves you gasping for air. Instead, it dulls, settles deep into your bones, becoming something you carry—not like a wound, but like a phantom limb, something that should not be there but still stays. That's what the days after losing her became—hollow, weightless, just a series of sunrises and sunsets that meant nothing to me.

I woke up each morning not because I wanted to, but because I had to. Life kept moving forward, indifferent to the wreckage it had left me in.

The world didn't stop spinning just because my heart had been shattered. Classes continued. People laughed. Conversations happened around me, voices rising and falling like background noise in a movie I no longer wanted to be a part of. The same corridors we once walked together now stood as mere pathways, stripped of the warmth they once held. I walked through them like a ghost, existing but not truly living.

I started keeping to myself more. The people around me noticed the change, but they never really understood it. How could they? They hadn't felt what I had felt, hadn't lost what I had lost. They hadn't known what it was like to hold the world in their hands one day and wake up the next to find it had slipped through their fingers like grains of sand.

They told me time heals all wounds, but time did nothing. *It only stretched the distance between what was and what is, making me feel further and further away from the life I once knew. Time did not soften the edges of my grief. It did not ease the weight on my chest. It only made me more aware of the absence, of how days turned into weeks, weeks into months, and yet nothing within me had changed.*

Her absence was everywhere. It was in the quiet spaces between conversations, where her voice should have been, filling the gaps with laughter, with warmth, with the effortless ease of knowing she was there.

Now, silence stretched between words like an open wound, raw and gaping, reminding me that something vital was missing. It was in the empty chair next to me in the cafeteria, a void that no one else could fill. I could still picture her sitting there, twirling a spoon between her fingers, softly playing with her hair while she talked about things that probably didn't matter to anyone else—but mattered to me.

Her absence was in the way I still reached for my phone instinctively, my fingers moving on their own as if muscle memory alone could bring her back. I would stop just before dialing her number, staring at the screen, heart pounding, knowing she wouldn't answer—knowing that even if she did, she wasn't mine to call anymore. It was in the songs I used to love but now couldn't bear to hear, the ones that had once been background music to our stolen moments, our late-night conversations, our shared silence that had always felt so full. Now, every note felt like a knife, every lyric like a cruel reminder of something I couldn't have back.

Her absence lived in the scent of a passing stranger that smelled just faintly like her perfume, making my breath hitch, making my heart race for a second before reality came crashing down. It was in the cold breeze that felt like her fingertips brushing against my skin. It was in the places we used to go; places I could no longer visit without feeling like a ghost walking through the ruins of what once was.

The coffee shop where we sat for hours, lost in conversations that felt like they could stretch on forever, was now just another building I avoided. The library where she used to lean her head against my shoulder, sighing in frustration over an assignment, now felt suffocating in its emptiness. Every street, every bench, every little corner of the world we once existed in together had turned into a graveyard of memories, each one a phantom that refused to let me be.

I kept telling myself that this was for the best, that maybe she was happier now, that maybe this was how things were meant to unfold.

But no matter how many times I whispered those words to myself, they never settled in my heart. They never felt true. Because late at night, when everything slowed down and I was left alone with nothing but the weight of my thoughts,

I couldn't shake off the questions that clawed at me. Did she ever miss me the way I missed her? Did she ever feel that same heaviness in her chest, the unbearable ache of absence, the suffocating quiet where something—someone—should have been? Did she ever stop in her tracks when something reminded her of me, her heart stuttering just for a moment before she forced herself to move on?

Did her fingers ever hesitate over my name in her contact list, just for a second, the way mine did every single day?

I tried to move on. I told myself that was what people did—they got up, they kept going, they put distance between themselves and the past until it no longer had the power to hurt them.

So, I forced myself to go out, to sit in circles that never quite felt like mine, to listen to conversations that never truly reached me. I laughed at jokes I didn't find funny, nodded along to stories I barely heard, pretending that I belonged. But no matter how much I tried to blend in, I always felt like a stranger among them, like I was standing behind a glass wall, watching a life that was supposed to be mine but no longer felt like it.

Nothing felt real anymore. The world around me continued to move, fast and unrelenting, but I felt stuck trapped in a version of myself that no longer fit.

The food I once loved tasted bland. The places I used to enjoy felt empty. Music, which had always been my escape, now felt like an open wound, every melody carrying traces of her, every lyric cutting a little deeper. Even time felt distorted—some days dragging on like an endless stretch of suffocating silence, others disappearing so fast I couldn't remember how I got from morning to night.

And then there was my reflection. I barely recognized the person staring back at me. The boy who used to wake up with excitement, who used to dream, who used to believe in something, was gone. In his place was someone unrecognizable—eyes sunken, devoid of the light they once carried, a smile that no longer reached them. I had memorized every inch of my own face, but it didn't feel like mine anymore. It felt like I was looking at a stranger, someone worn down by grief, someone I didn't know how to be.

I tried to move on. I really did. But moving on wasn't just about pretending to be okay in front of others. It wasn't about distractions, about keeping busy, about laughing when I wanted to cry. Moving on meant learning to live without her, and that was something I didn't know how to do.

I started writing, not because I wanted to, but because it was the only way I could scream without making a sound. The words poured out of me like spilled ink, bleeding onto the pages with a grief that refused to be contained. I wrote about her, about us, about the way love can feel like the most beautiful thing in the world and then turn into the very thing that destroys you. I wrote about the way she once looked at me like I was the only thing in the world that mattered, and how now, I had become nothing more than a stranger to her. I wrote until my hands ached, until my eyes blurred with unshed tears, until I could finally breathe again, if only for a moment.

But no matter how much I wrote, no matter how many cigarettes I smoked or how many drinks I downed, nothing changed the fact that she was gone. And she wasn't coming back.

I could pour my grief onto every page, bleed out my pain in ink, let every word carry the weight of my longing—but she would never read them. I could write until my hands ached, until my thoughts unraveled into poetry, but words wouldn't bring her back. They couldn't summon the warmth of her laughter; couldn't recreate the way she used to look at me when she thought I wasn't watching. No sentence, no metaphor, no desperate plea scrawled in the margins of my notebook could reach her now.

I could drown myself in alcohol, let it burn my throat, let it flood my veins, hoping it would erase her from my system. But the moment the high faded, the moment my mind cleared, she was still there etched into my bones, whispering through the silence. The cigarettes I smoked didn't cloud her memory; they only made my lungs as heavy as my heart. I exhaled smoke, but never the pain. I tried to suffocate the love I had for her, but love like this didn't die—it dwelled, unshaken, unyielding, refusing to be destroyed.

I tried everything—every form of escape, every method of forgetting—but the truth remained the same. She was gone. She had chosen a life without me in it, and no amount of self-destruction could change that.

I wake, I breathe, I move, I fade,
A hollow life, a love unmade.
The echoes whisper through the night,
A name once bright, now lost in light.

I trace the paths we used to roam,
Footsteps remain, yet I'm alone.
The walls still hold her laughter's sound,
But silence weighs where she was found.

The sky still turns from black to gold,
Yet every dawn feels bleak and cold.
The sun may rise, the birds may sing,
But none of it revives a thing.

The seasons shift, the leaves still fall,
Yet nothing changes, not at all.
The streets still breathe, the world still turns,
Yet deep inside, my sorrow burns.

I walk through days I don't belong,
The faces blur, the voices wrong.
They talk, they smile, they live, they shine,
But none of it feels real to mine.

Time moves on, but I stay still,
A ghost who walks against his will.
Trapped between the past and now,
A love once sworn, a broken vow.

I search for meaning in the gray,
For something left, a reason to stay.
Yet all I find is empty space,
A life untouched by her embrace.

And so, I write, and so I drown,
In words, in smoke, in endless rounds.
Each letter spills the pain I hide,
Yet nothing heals this loss inside.

The Ghost of Her & Unfinished Conversations

She never truly left.

Not in the way people assume when love fades and memories dissolve. She was never just a name I used to know or a face that blurred into the past.

No, she remained—woven into the fabric of my existence, existing in the quiet spaces of my mind, whispering through the wind on lonely nights.

She was in the songs that played in coffee shops, the ones I used to send her at 2 a.m. because I thought she'd love the lyrics as much as I did.

She was in the empty seat beside me on the bus, the one she used to lean against, half asleep, her hair brushing my shoulder. She was in the places we once called 'ours'—the campus bench under the winter sky, the dimly lit street where we walked in silence, the canteen where she stole bites from my plate like it was the most natural thing in the world.

She lived in my routines. In the way I picked up my phone and almost typed her name before stopping myself. In the way I still looked for her in crowded places, half-expecting her to be there, half-hoping she wasn't.

Because if she was there, it would remind me that she was happy without me, and if she wasn't, it would remind me that she was gone. Either way, it would hurt.

The worst part? The conversations that never truly ended. The ones that still played in my head, over and over, like a broken record I couldn't turn off.

I wanted to ask her—why? Why did she let go when I was holding on with everything I had? Why did she let people decide our fate when we knew each other better than anyone? Why did she walk away, knowing that I was still standing there, waiting for her to turn around?

But I never asked.

Not because I didn't want to. Not because I didn't have a million questions clawing at my throat every time, I saw her. But because deep down, I knew the answers wouldn't change anything. I knew she had her reasons, and I knew they would never be enough to fill the void she left.

So, instead, we talked about nothing.

Conversations became polite and empty.

"How have you been?" she would ask, and I'd lie. *"I'm good. You?"*

She would nod, smile— *"Yeah, good."*

And that was it. That was all we allowed ourselves to say, as if pretending we were fine would somehow make it true.

But the unsaid things screamed louder than words ever could. I wanted to tell her that I wasn't okay. That I still reached for my phone in the middle of the night, hoping for a message that would never come. That I still rewrote our story in my head, trying to find the moment where I could have changed everything. That I still dreamed about her, and in my dreams, she still looked at me the way she used to—like I was her home.

But she wasn't the same, and neither was I.

I saw it in her eyes—the hesitation, the guarded walls that weren't there before. There was a time when I could read every thought behind those eyes, when she would look at me and I'd know exactly what she was feeling.

But now, she was a stranger wearing the face of someone I once loved

more than life itself. And maybe that was the cruelest part of it all.

We still existed in the same world, breathed the same air, walked the same streets. But the distance between us was infinite.

We were close enough to see each other, but too far to touch.

Close enough to hear each other's voices, but too distant to say the things that truly mattered.

The ghost of her followed me everywhere, haunting me in the quiet moments, in the spaces between words, in the pauses between breaths.

And no matter how much I tried to silence it, it stayed.

Because the truth is, I didn't want to let her go.

Letting go would mean accepting that she was never coming back. Letting go would mean erasing the idea of 'us' that I had held onto for so long. Letting go would mean admitting that love doesn't always win, that sometimes, despite everything, people walk away.

And maybe that was the hardest part.

Because I wasn't ready to say goodbye, even if she already had.

She echoes in the hush of dawn,
A whisper wrapped in golden light,
A name that time has tried to fade,
Yet clings to me with quiet might.

I see her in the autumn breeze,
In echoes of a distant song,
She lives in every empty seat,
In places where we both belonged.

I hear her laugh where silence grows,
In echoes caught in midnight air,
A voice that time should steal away,
Yet somehow, still, it's always there.

I reach for her in crowded streets,
A phantom touch, a hollow trace,
My hands close on a fleeting dream,
But find no warmth, no soft embrace.

She left, but never fully gone,
Her ghost still whispers, soft and slow,
Not in the way that ghosts should be—
She haunts in ways she doesn't know.

I wonder if she feels it too,
The pull of moments left unsaid,
Does she recall the quiet nights,
Or do I haunt her heart instead?

But ghosts don't speak, and nor do we,
So I will let the echoes fade,
And love her in the space between,
Where dreams and memories are made.

The Weight of Memories & Loving a Shadow

Memories are strange things. They live inside you, even when you wish they wouldn't. Some are gentle, like a whisper of the past that caresses your soul, while others claw at your chest, demanding to be felt, no matter how much time has passed.

With her, the memories weren't just passing moments—they were entire lifetimes trapped inside my mind, refusing to let me go.

Every little thing carried her presence. The scent of winter air on my skin reminded me of the nights we spent walking under the quiet sky, where words weren't needed because our silences were enough.

The sight of certain books on a shelf, ones she once mentioned in passing, sent waves of nostalgia crashing over me, forcing me to remember how she spoke about them with a passion that made me love them even before I turned a single page.

Even music—especially became unbearable.

I used to find solace in songs, but now they only carried echoes of a voice that wasn't mine, laughter that wasn't meant for me anymore.

Moving on was never about forgetting.

It was about carrying the weight of her absence and learning to breathe despite it. But some days, the weight was too much—too heavy, too suffocating, pressing down on my chest until every breath felt like a battle, I wasn't sure I wanted to win.

Some days, it felt like I was standing on the edge of the past, reaching for a hand that had already let go, fingers closing around nothing but air and memories that refused to fade.

There were mornings when I woke up with the ghost of her name on my lips, only to realize that saying it out loud wouldn't bring her back.

Afternoons where I walked through familiar streets, seeing her everywhere and nowhere all at once.

Evenings where I stared at my phone, scrolling mindlessly, convincing myself I wouldn't check if she was online—but always giving in, always hoping for something that never came.

And then there were the nights. The cruelest of them all. Nights where I lay in the dark, replaying every conversation, every touch, every glance that had once felt like a promise.

Nights where I swore, I could still hear her laughter if I closed my eyes tightly enough.

Nights where I told myself I was moving on, but deep down, I knew I was still waiting.

Because moving on wasn't about forgetting.

It wasn't about erasing her from the story of my life. It was about learning to exist in a world where she no longer did. It was about carrying her absence like an ache that never truly healed, learning to walk forward even as my heart kept turning back.

And some days, that was the hardest thing of all.

And then, there was the realization.

The painful, gut-wrenching truth that crept into my soul when I least expected it—the kind of truth that doesn't hit you all at once but seeps in slowly, like poison in the bloodstream.

It came in quiet moments, in the pauses between thoughts, in the stillness of nights when I could no longer drown myself in distractions.

I wasn't in love with her anymore.

I was in love with who she was when she was with me.

Or maybe, more truthfully, I was in love with who I thought she was. I was in love with the way she made me feel—like I mattered, like I was enough, like I was someone worth holding on to.

I was in love with the comfort of her presence, the way she fit so effortlessly into the empty spaces of my life, the way she made the world feel a little less lonely.

I was in love with the way she looked at me, like I was something irreplaceable, even if just for a brief moment. But that moment had passed. And she wasn't that person anymore.

Or maybe she never was.

Maybe I had only fallen for the version of her that I created in my mind—the girl who saw me the way I wanted to be seen, who needed me the way I needed her, who stayed even when the world told her to leave.

Maybe I had turned her into something she was never meant to be—an anchor in the storm, a home in the chaos, a love that would last beyond reason.

But she wasn't my anchor. She wasn't my home. And love, no matter how deep, no matter how desperate, was never enough to make someone stay.

So, I sat with this truth, letting it settle into the cracks of my heart, letting it hurt the way all endings do. Because sometimes, the hardest thing to accept isn't that someone left—it's realizing that maybe, just maybe, they were never really there to begin with.

Loving a shadow is the cruelest form of love. It's loving an echo, a trace of someone who once was, but no longer is.

It's reaching into the past, grasping at something intangible, something already gone, convincing yourself that if you just try harder, if you just love stronger, if you just refuse to let go—maybe, just maybe—it will be enough to bring her back.

But shadows don't return love.

Shadows don't hold your hand in the quiet moments, don't lean their head against your shoulder when the weight of the world feels too heavy.

Shadows don't whisper your name in the dark, don't send you songs at 2 a.m. just because they remind them of you. Shadows don't stay. They linger, they haunt, but they don't stay.

And so, I lived with the ghost of a girl who was no longer mine. A girl who had moved forward while I remained stuck in a loop of memories, rewinding, replaying, reliving.

Every street we walked together became a cemetery of moments frozen in time. Every place we once called ours now felt like a cruel reminder of what had been and what would never be again.

I told myself she was happy now. That she had found the kind of love she deserved, the kind of love I couldn't give, or maybe the kind of love she had never wanted from me in the first place.

But even knowing that, I couldn't stop missing her. Missing not just who she was, but who I was when I was with her.

They say time heals everything. But what if I don't want to be healed?

What if the wound is all I have left of her? Because to heal would mean to forget, to let her slip away completely. And as much as it hurt, as much as it hollowed me out from the inside, I wasn't ready for that.

Maybe I never would be.

She drifts within the quiet nights,
A whisper carved in hollow light.
She walks in echoes down my spine,
A phantom love that once was mine.

She lives in pages torn and frayed,
In letters inked but never made.
Her laughter hums in silent air,
A melody that isn't there.

I see her in the winter's breath,
In sunsets bleeding into death.
In coffee left to turn ice-cold,
In stories that will not grow old.

She stays in spaces left untouched,
In hands I once had known too much.
In places where we used to be,
In love that only I can see.

Perhaps I loved a dream too bright,
A star that burned into the night.
For when I reach, when I react,
I find the ghost who loved me back.

FAREWELL MEMORIES

The final days of college felt like the slow unraveling of a dream I had held onto for too long. I knew this moment was coming—the moment where life would demand I move forward, leaving behind the place that had given me both the best and the worst memories of my life. But knowing didn't make it easier. Nothing could have made it easier.

The campus was alive with bittersweet goodbyes. Friends clung to each other, making promises they knew deep down would be hard to keep. Yearbooks filled with scribbled messages, shirts covered in ink, and eyes that shimmered with unshed tears—it was the end of an era, the final chapter of a story we had spent years writing.

But while everyone around me celebrated, I felt like I was watching it all from the outside, a silent observer in a moment that should have meant something more.

There was a space on my shirt that I had left untouched, right over my heart. It wasn't accidental. It wasn't random. It was waiting—waiting for words from the only person whose message would truly matter. As others came and wrote their goodbyes, their inside jokes, their well-wishes, I barely registered any of it. My mind was elsewhere. My heart was elsewhere.

And then, she picked up a pen.

For a moment, I held my breath as she placed her hand on my shirt, her fingers just barely brushing against the fabric. It was a strange thing, how something so small could feel like everything. A moment stretched in time, a moment where I dared to believe she might say more, write more—leave behind something

I could carry with me, something that would tell me I still mattered to her.

But when she stepped back, all she had written was:

"Once upon a time waale favorite senior."

That was all.

I stared at the words, letting them settle into the space I had so carefully saved for her. They felt like a whisper, like a door closing softly instead of slamming shut. Not a confession. Not a regret. Just a memory, frozen in ink.

It wasn't what I had hoped for. It wasn't enough. But it was something. A fragile thread between what we were and what we had become.

And maybe that was all we were ever meant to be—just a story from once upon a time.

But words on fabric could never replace what I truly wanted—a moment, a memory, something that felt real. So, I called her, asked her to meet me one last time before I left. I knew this might be the last time I'd see her; the last time I'd have a chance to say everything my heart had been holding in.

She came.

And in that moment, nothing else mattered. Not the past, not the pain, not even the unspoken words that had built a wall between us. *It was just her, standing in front of me, looking at me the way she always had—like I was someone who once meant something to her. Like I was someone who maybe, just maybe, still did.*

I had planned to give her something—memories, pieces of my heart wrapped in small tokens. Things I had saved for her birthday, gifts that never reached her hands because of everything that had come between us. Now, they no longer felt like presents but parting gifts. A way to leave behind something of me, even if I couldn't stay.

I placed them in her hands, watching as she held them with a softness that made my chest tighten.

For a moment, she didn't say anything. She just traced her fingers over the wrapping, as if memorizing the weight of something she wasn't sure she wanted to carry. As if trying to decide whether accepting them meant accepting the love I had poured into them.

There was a sadness in her eyes. A reflection of my own. I wanted to believe that the tears forming in her gaze were for me, for us, for everything that could have been. That maybe she, too, was standing in the wreckage of what we once were, unsure of how to walk away.

But I wasn't sure. *And I didn't dare ask.*

Because the answer might have shattered me completely.

So, we just stood there, two people caught between what was and what would never be.

She looked at me, and I looked at her, both of us standing on the edge of something we could never step into. *There were words I wanted to say, but they felt useless. What could I say that hadn't already been felt? What could I ask when I already knew the answers?*

And yet, I spoke anyway. Because I had to. Because I needed her to know.

"I'll wait," I told her. Because it was the only truth I had left. ***"No matter what happens."***

She shook her head, a sad smile playing on her lips.

"No one waits. Everyone moves on."

I didn't argue. Because how could I explain that my heart wasn't built like everyone else's? That love, for me, wasn't something destructible, something that faded with time or distance?

How could I tell her that she had carved her name so deeply into my soul that even if I tried to erase it, the imprint would remain? That I could live an entire lifetime carrying her love without expecting anything in return? That even if she walked away, she would always be the only home my heart knew?

So, I let the silence speak for me.

And then, I left.

I left the college that had given me her. The place where I had first seen her name light up my phone screen, where I had fallen in love with the way she existed so effortlessly, where I had stayed even when it hurt—just to be close to her.

And I left the college that had taken her away from me. The same place that had made me realize that love is not always enough, that timing is cruel, that sometimes, no matter how much you give, it will never be yours to keep.

The road ahead was waiting, a future calling out to me. There were new beginnings to be made, new people to meet, new memories to create. Everyone said so.

But what no one understood was that I wasn't looking for any of it. My heart wasn't searching for a fresh start—it was searching for the pieces of her that I might find in the in-between moments of my life. And with every step away, I felt like I was walking in the wrong direction. *Like I was leaving behind the only thing that ever truly felt like home.*

So, I carried her with me. In the echoes of her laughter that played in my mind like an old song I could never forget.

In the ghost of her touch that kept feeling on my skin, in the way my fingers twitched as if still reaching for hers. In the spaces of my heart that would forever belong to her, untouched and unclaimed by anyone else. Because love doesn't end when someone leaves.

It stays. And sometimes, it becomes the

very thing that keeps you alive.

I left the college, but you stayed in my heart,
In the ink of your words, in the place torn apart.
A farewell written, yet nothing was said,
A love unfinished, a path left unread.

I watched you smile as I walked away,
Wondering if you'd call, if you'd ask me to stay.
But silence stood where love should have been,
And I disappeared in the spaces between.

I gave you memories wrapped in time,
Hoping you'd keep them as I kept mine.
Did they weigh on your hands like they did in my chest?
Or were they just remnants of a past you left?

Tears in your eyes or was it just a dream?
A moment too brief, slipping like a stream.
I told you I'd wait, though you didn't believe,
But love doesn't vanish—it only weaves.

I left, but I never left you behind,
In the whispers of wind, in the echoes of time.
And if love could transcend this life we are in,
Then maybe, just maybe, I'd find you again.

In another time, in another place,
Where love isn't lost in the hands of fate.
Where I don't have to leave, where you don't walk away,
And forever isn't just something we say.

A New City, The Same Heart

When I started working, my company gave me the option to work from home. At first, it felt like a blessing—a slow transition from college life into the real world, a chance to settle into the next phase of life without abrupt changes. But soon, I realized it was a curse in disguise.

For five to six months, I worked from home, keeping myself occupied during the day. My priorities were clear—I never let my emotions interfere with my work. But once the laptop screen went dark and the silence of my room took over, there was only one thing left in my mind: her.

I was stuck. Even today, I wonder if I ever truly moved forward.

Then, time moved forward, and so did she.

I heard the news—she had started dating the same guy I had once mentioned. I had known this would happen. Somewhere deep inside, I had already prepared myself for it. And yet, when the moment arrived, it still broke me. It still shattered something within me.

But instead of letting that pain turn into resentment, I held onto love. I still believed, still hoped, still waited—despite knowing I was waiting for something that was never meant to happen. Instead of *hating her, I loved her more.*

It would be easy for someone to misunderstand her place in this story. But love does not need a villain — it only needs truth. And the truth is, she was one of the most beautiful souls I've ever known. If anything, she was the light in a world that often felt too dark, the calm in the middle of the storm I never knew I would have to weather alone.

She is one of the best people I have ever met—perhaps the best. Not because she was perfect, but because she was real.

She was the kind of person stories should be written about—not as a cautionary tale, not as a tragic chapter, but as a testament to what it means to be truly beautiful, inside and out. I could fill endless pages about the kind of soul she carried—one that was kind in ways that mattered, warm in ways that felt like home, and full of peace in a world that so often felt restless. She had a heart that understood a presence that comforted, and a way of existing that made the world seem a little softer, a little kinder.

She wasn't just someone you date for the thrill of it; she was someone you date to marry. She was the kind of person you build a life with, the kind you cherish, the kind you hold onto if you're lucky enough. She wasn't meant for temporary love; she was meant for something lasting, something deep, something true.

And in a world as chaotic as this, she was the kind of peace I had always longed for—the kind of peace I would have spent a lifetime protecting, if only I had the chance.

But despite all the love I carried for her, it was getting too heavy. So, I decided to leave.

I moved to Bangalore, hoping that a new city, new people, and new experiences would help me move on. At first, it was lonely. I had no friends here, no familiar faces to ease the weight of change. Days felt long, nights felt longer. I was merely passing time, waiting for something—anything—to make me feel different.

Then, slowly, I started meeting people. I made friends. I began stepping out more, engaging in conversations that weren't tied to my past. For the first time in a long while, I felt a small, distant hope. Maybe this was it. Maybe this was the beginning of moving on.

But no matter how much I tried, she never truly left. We were still in touch, though not like before. She reached out sometimes—mostly when she needed to be uplifted. And every time her name appeared on my screen; it was as if time folded in on itself. Her words pulled me back into the past, into a version of myself I was trying to leave behind. One message, one conversation, and suddenly, I was back to where I started.

The office I stepped into wasn't just a workplace—*it was a space woven with the remnants of dreams we once shared. When we were in college, we often spoke about the future, about how she would work hard and land a job in the same company as mine.* It wasn't just a plan; it was a promise we silently held between us—a dream of growing together, of standing side by side as we built our careers.

And now, here I was. But she wasn't.

Yet, I knew—somewhere deep inside her heart—that dream still existed. Even today, a part of her might still want to walk through these same hallways, to share lunch breaks, to turn those late-night conversations about the future into a reality. Maybe she never said it out loud, but I could feel it. And maybe that's what made it even harder.

Memories of her were everywhere. In the smallest corners, in the most unexpected moments. *In the way I grabbed my coffee and remembered how she liked hers. In the way I sat at my desk, wondering how it would feel if she were at the one next to mine.* In the way, certain words, certain meetings, certain dates on the calendar pulled me back to a time when she and I spoke about this life like it was ours to share.

And I loved those memories. I lived in them. I breathed them in.

Every day, I wasn't just moving forward—I was falling deeper into the past. Falling for the echoes of a love that was never mine to keep. Falling for the moments that never made it beyond 'what could have been.'

Moving forward felt like trying to climb out of quicksand. Every step ahead was followed by another pull backward. And I wondered—was it truly possible to move on from a love like this? Or was I destined to carry her with me, no matter where life took me next?

Switching my job felt like my last attempt to escape her presence, or at least the echoes of it that haunted me in that office. I had chosen Bangalore to move on, to start fresh, but instead, I had carried her with me into every aspect of my new life. The office, the very place where I should have been focused on work and growth, became another place where she lingered.

We had spoken about this once, back in college. How she would work hard, how we would end up in the same company, in the same city, living out the plans we had woven in the late hours of conversations that once felt like promises. And yet, here I was—alone. Walking through hallways we had imagined walking together. Sitting at a desk where I had once envisioned her beside me, our lunch breaks filled with laughter and unspoken dreams.

I couldn't do it anymore.

The thing I had come running from—her memories, the ache of her absence—was getting hold of me even more in this place.

So, I did what felt like the only option. I switched my job. I packed up my feelings and moved to another workplace, hoping that maybe, just maybe, distance would finally bring peace.

For a while, I felt a bit more relaxed. The reminders weren't as sharp. But it didn't take long for my mind to betray me again.

Because the thing about memories is that they don't need places to exist. They live within you. They follow you into new cities, new routines, new moments that were supposed to belong to someone else but still held her name.

Every street I walked down, I imagined her beside me. The city was unfamiliar, the roads nameless in my mind, the people strangers passing by without meaning. Yet, in the midst of all that unfamiliarity, she was the only thing that felt real. It was almost instinctual—the way my mind filled in the empty spaces with her presence, as if she had never left.

I saw her in the way my footsteps fell in sync with someone else's, as if she were walking beside me. I imagined the way she would tilt her head, squinting at a signboard with that curious expression she always had when trying to read something from a distance. I could hear her voice, the way she would tug at my sleeve and say, *'Look at that place, we have to go there someday.'* And in my head, I always answered, *'Yes, we will.'* But the words never left my lips because there was no one beside me to hear them.

The city was alive, buzzing with lights and endless possibilities, yet I walked through it with a heart still trapped in the past. Every café I stepped into alone, I talked to her in my mind. The moment I entered, I instinctively glanced around, as if searching for a familiar pair of eyes, as if she would somehow already be there, waiting for me like she used to. I ordered coffee, the same one she liked, just to feel closer to her, to pretend, if only for a few minutes, that nothing had changed.

I pictured her across the table, stirring her drink in that absentminded way she always did, watching the swirl of coffee as if it held the answers to all her thoughts. I could almost hear her voice, teasing me about how I always took my coffee too strong, how she would steal sips from my cup just to make a face at how bitter it was.

The world saw me sitting alone, but in my head, she was there smiling, talking, existing in a way that made my solitude feel less empty.

But then the moment would break. A waiter would place the cup in front of me, and the reality would hit me like a cruel reminder—there was no one sitting across from me. There was no one stirring her coffee, no one stealing glances at me between conversations, No one reaching across the table to touch my hand without a second thought.

Just an empty chair, just a one-sided conversation, just a love that still lived in my mind, even when she had long since walked away. And then came the question that had haunted me for so long—
Had I gone mad in love?

But if this wasn't love, then what was?

It wasn't about madness. It wasn't about obsession. It was about the extent to which I had explored what love could make a person feel.

Love wasn't just an emotion anymore—it had become my existence. It was no longer just a momentary feeling that came and went; it was woven into my very being, shaping the way I moved through the world.

It had altered the way I breathed, turning every exhale into a whisper of her name, every inhale into a silent prayer that maybe, just maybe, she still carried a fragment of me within her. It had changed the way I saw the world—not through my own eyes, but through the lens of what we could have been, what we should have been. Every place held a possibility, every moment an echo of something I wished had happened.

Love had become the invisible weight I carried, the quiet presence that followed me even when I was alone. *It had made me realize that some people aren't just a part of your life—they become your life.* They redefine your sense of purpose, your understanding of happiness, your very identity. And that's what she had done to me.

Love was not just something I felt—it was something I lived. It was a presence, a shadow, a heartbeat that refused to slow down, even when there was no one left to hear it. But even love—no matter how deep—can become exhausting. So, I found the easiest way out.

I started going to clubs, throwing myself into the nightlife of the city. If distractions couldn't come naturally, I would force them. I partied when I needed to, surrounded myself with music, drinks, and crowds that blurred reality. I convinced myself that if I just kept moving, if I just kept meeting people, the void inside me would eventually fill itself.

And for a moment, it felt like it was working.

I talked to new people, let conversations flow, even entertained the idea of moving forward with someone else and tried. I told myself that she wasn't the only girl in the world, that there were others who could maybe, someday, make me feel something again.

But it took only a few conversations and meetings to realize the truth.

None of them touched even a fraction of my soul. Conversations felt scripted, predictable—just words spoken into the air without meaning, without weight. Their laughter didn't echo in my mind the way hers did, their presence didn't stir anything deep within me. They sat across from me, talked, smiled, shared stories, but it all felt distant, as if I was merely playing a role in a life that wasn't mine.

I was there, but I wasn't there. I was listening, but not really listening. My heart wasn't in the present; it was still lost somewhere in the past, still tethered to the girl who once made the world feel alive.

No matter how hard I tried, I couldn't see them the way I saw her. Their eyes didn't hold the same universe, their voices didn't carry the same warmth. There was no depth, no familiarity, no sense of home. Every small gesture reminded me of her absence—how she used to tilt her head while listening, how she would absentmindedly play with the edge of her sleeves, how she knew the weight of my silences without me having to explain. With her, everything had meaning. With them, everything felt like noise.

I couldn't bring myself to look at them with the same admiration, the same quiet longing that had once been reserved for her. My heart refused to open; my soul refused to recognize anyone else as its own. And in that moment, I understood something I had been denying all along—There was no way I could move on from her.

This wasn't about time or distractions, about meeting someone new or forcing myself to feel something that wasn't there. This was something deeper, something unchangeable. She wasn't just a chapter in my past; she was the ink that had rewritten my entire story. Moving on wasn't a choice, because moving on would mean erasing something that had become a part of me. And I knew, with every breath, every heartbeat, that I wasn't ready for that.

Maybe I never would be.

She wasn't just another girl. She wasn't just another name in the past.

She was the girl. The kind of person who ruins you for everyone else, not because they shattered you, but because they set a standard so high, so untouchable, that no one else could ever reach it. She wasn't just another love story—she was the love story, the one that redefined the very meaning of love for me. She didn't just exist in my life; she reshaped it, leaving behind an imprint so deep that even time struggled to erase it.

She was the one who made love feel effortless, yet all-consuming. The one who didn't just fit into my world—she became my world. With her, conversations weren't just words exchanged; they were moments woven with meaning. Her presence wasn't just something I enjoyed; it was something I needed. She had this quiet way of making everything feel lighter, of making the ordinary seem extraordinary, of making me believe that love wasn't just a passing feeling, but something tangible, something real, something worth holding onto.

She was *too* perfect in my eyes—not in the sense of flawlessness, but in the way she was *perfect for me*. The way she understood my silences, the way she laughed at my worst jokes, the way she saw me in ways no one else ever had. It was in the way she carried herself, the way she cared so deeply about the little things, the way she made even the most chaotic moments feel peaceful.

She was *irreplaceable*. Not because I hadn't met other people, but because no one else could ever come close. No one else could speak in the language of my soul the way she did. No one else could stand beside me and make the world feel right. No one else had the same depth in their eyes, the same warmth in their voice, the same quiet magic in their presence.

She was too deeply etched into my being. Not just as a memory, but as a feeling, a presence that refused to fade. She wasn't just someone I loved—she became a part of me, interwoven into the very fabric of my existence. And no matter how much time passed, no matter where life took me, I knew one thing with certainty: she would always be *the* girl. The one who changed everything. And so, I was stuck again.

A new city. New people. A new job.

But the same aching heart.

And the worst part? She wasn't even there.

Yet, she was everywhere.

I met new faces, I heard new names,
But none of them set my soul aflame.
None of them carried the warmth in their voice,
None of them felt like the right choice.

They spoke, they laughed, they stood by my side,
But with every word, I felt more confined.
Because love was never meant to be forced,
And my heart still wandered back to its source.

She was the girl, the only one,
The kind you don't forget, not even once.
Not because she left me torn apart,
But because she loved me in ways that stayed in my heart.

She was the face in every crowded street,
The echo in footsteps, the ghost in my seat.
She was the voice I still longed to hear,
The absence that made the world unclear.

I searched for her in every new place,
In the eyes of another, in a stranger's embrace.
But no one carried the depth in their gaze,
No one could match the love in her ways.

A Prayer for the Girl Who Was Never Mine

I was never the kind of person who believed in God.

Not after my father's death. Not after I learned that prayers don't bring back the people you love, that whispered wishes don't rewrite fate. I had seen too much loss, too much silence in the face of suffering, to believe in divine intervention. I convinced myself that life was nothing but a string of coincidences, a series of random events that had no grand design.

I never looked for meaning in prayers. I never found comfort in temples, in churches, in mosques—I found only quiet spaces where people begged for things that were never promised to them. And I swore I would never be one of them. I would never let myself fall into the illusion that someone was listening, that destiny could be changed.

But then, I lost her.

And suddenly, the only faith I had left—the only thing that could ever bring her back—was God and manifestation.

I don't know when it started. Maybe it was the first night after I left college, lying in my room, staring at the ceiling, whispering her name into the dark as if the universe might hear me.

Maybe it was when I scrolled through old conversations, rereading them like prayers, searching for signs I had missed. Maybe it was the moment I realized that no force on this earth—not logic, not time, not even love itself—could change her mind. The only thing left to believe in was something beyond this world.

So, I did the one thing I never thought I would do.

I started praying.

Every religious place I visited, every shrine, every temple, every mosque—I carried her name with me. I didn't bow my head for myself.

I didn't pray for success, for happiness, for peace. I prayed for her. I prayed for us. I prayed that somehow, the impossible could be rewritten.

That fate, which had been so cruel, would find a way to bring her back into my life.

Every time I made a wish, every time I stood in front of something sacred, I manifested us. I closed my eyes and pictured a future where we were together, where she chose me, where life gave us another chance.

I imagined waking up one day to a message from her, imagined seeing her walk toward me on a random street, imagined hearing her say the words I had waited so long to hear: I was wrong. I should have stayed.

I convinced myself that if she ever came back to me, if God made this impossible love story real again, then I would start believing.

I would surrender to the idea that some things are meant to be, that prayers are heard, that destiny does have a way of bringing back what is truly ours.

But if she didn't?

If she never came back, if no miracle happened, if every wish, every folded hand, every desperate plea was ignored—then I would know.

I would know that God doesn't exist. That fate is just an illusion. That love is nothing more than a cruel trick the universe plays on the hopeless.

This was my test. My gamble with faith.

And so, I waited.

I waited for a sign, for a message, for something—anything—to tell me that my prayers weren't in vain. That somewhere, in some corner of her heart, she still thought of me the way I thought of her.

But days passed. Then weeks. Then months.

She didn't come back.

She didn't change her mind.

She didn't hear the prayers I sent out into the universe.

Still, I wasn't ready to stop believing. Not yet.

Because what if?

What if destiny was just waiting for the right time? What if fate was still writing our ending?

What if God was watching, testing my patience, seeing how much I was willing to wait?

So, I waited more.

I prayed harder.

I let my heart believe in something I never had faith in before— *miracles.*

Because if she was meant to be my destiny, then one day, life would bring her back to me.

And if not?

Then my destiny would be to love her in silence, to carry her with me in every lifetime that follows this one.

Either way, I knew one thing—I could never stop loving her. Not in this life. Not in the next. Not even in the ones after that.

I never believed, but now I do,
Not in gods, but prayers for you.
Not in fate, but whispered pleas,
Begging stars and silent trees.

I light a candle, say your name,
Hoping heaven bends its game.
Hoping winds will change their tune,
Hoping love can bring you soon.

If you return, then faith is true,
That miracles can pull me through.
But if you stay a distant dream,
Then faith is just a cruel routine.

So here I stand, my hands still raised,
Praying for the love we'd saved.
Praying, though my heart still knows,
Some prayers bloom, while others go.

I kneel before the night's embrace,
Not seeking mercy, just a trace.
A sign, a shift, a fleeting spark,
A whisper breaking through the dark.

I carve your name in quiet air,
Send it drifting, send it there.
To skies that stole you far from me,
To time that laughs at what could be.

If love alone could bend the tide,
I'd pull you back, stand by your side.
But love is light, and time is stone,
And prayers can't bring back what's gone.

Yet still, I beg, yet still, I wait,
Defying time, defying fate.
For if not this life, then the next,
Where love won't fade, nor go unkept.

A Love That Was Never Temporary

I never wanted her to be just a passing moment—something transient, something that arrives like a whisper and fades like an echo. I never wanted her to be any sort of an insignificant chapter in my life, a story I'd outgrow, a memory that time would dull. I wanted her to be the story itself—the pages, the ink, the unwritten future that stretched beyond endings

I wanted a *future* with her.

I wanted to wake up next to her years from now, in a home that felt like *us*—a home filled with memories, where every corner carried echoes of laughter, where the walls had witnessed countless late-night conversations and quiet, stolen moments of love.

A home that smelled like freshly brewed coffee in the mornings, the soft aroma of vanilla candles in the evenings, and the comforting scent of books we had collected over the years—stories we had lived, stories we had yet to read, stories we had written together in the pages of our own life.

I wanted to build a life where love wasn't just a passing emotion, something fragile and mortal, but a foundation—strong, unshakable, unwavering and immortal.

A love that wasn't measured in grand gestures but in the little things—her sleepy voice in the mornings, the way she'd hum to herself while cooking, the way our fingers would always find their way to each other's even in the middle of a crowded street.

I wanted a love that stood the test of time, where even after decades, she would still be the first thought that crossed my mind in the morning and the last prayer I whispered to the universe before I slept.

I wanted to grow old with her.

To watch the seasons change, the years pass, and still feel the same warmth in her touch as I did when we first met. I wanted to sit beside her on quiet evenings, where words weren't always necessary because our silences spoke just as much.

To laugh over things that no one else would understand—inside jokes we had collected over time, stories from our youth that we never got tired of telling, dreams we had once chased and the beautiful life we had built instead.

I wanted to hold her hands as they wrinkled with time, to trace the same fingers I had once intertwined with mine in our younger days.

I wanted to watch her face age gracefully, to see the fine lines at the corners of her eyes deepen, not as signs of time passing, but as proof that we had *lived*—that we had smiled, loved, and shared a lifetime of happiness together.

I wanted to look at her, years down the line, and still see the same light in her eyes that I had fallen for—the same spark, the same quiet beauty, the same soul that had made me believe in love in the first place.

Because I never wanted a love that ended.

I wanted *forever.*

And forever, in my heart, she will always be.

I never wanted something that would come and go. I never wanted a love with an expiration date.

I wanted her *till the end.*

But sometimes, love does not ask what we want.

It gives, it takes, and it leaves us with the pieces of what could have been.

And now, I will carry those pieces forever.

I never sought a love that fades,
A moment's touch, a phase that sways.
I never wished for something brief,
A story lost like autumn's leaf.

I dreamed of mornings warm and bright,
Her laughter soft, the golden light.
A home that hummed with whispered dreams,
Where love still lived in quiet seams.

Not measured in the grand and loud,
But in the way our hands had found,
Each other's touch in crowded space,
A silent vow, a sacred place.

To age with her, to watch time weave,
The years that love refused to leave.
To see the lines upon her face,
Not as decay, but time embraced.

But love is cruel in how it stays,
A shadow cast on hollow days.
It gave, it took, it set me free,
Yet left her name inside of me.

A Love That Was Never About Possession

I never wanted to *acquire* her. I never saw love as something to own, something to hold onto so tightly that it lost its essence. Love, to me, was never about claiming someone—it was about *cherishing* them.

I did not need labels. I did not need a title that the world could recognize. I only needed *her presence.*

Her presence alone was enough to make me happier than any sort of relationship with anyone else ever could. I did not need her to be *mine* in the way the world defines love.

I did not need a label, a promise, or even a future together. Just knowing that she walked this earth, that she was out there somewhere—laughing, living, dreaming—was enough to bring me peace.

I found comfort in the thought that she was waking up to sunrises just like I was, that she was looking up at the same moon on sleepless nights, that she was breathing under the same sky that stretched endlessly between us. She didn't have to be near me.

She didn't have to think of me. She only had to exist, and that was enough to make my heart a little lighter.

I didn't want her as a trophy, as a possession, as something bound by expectation. Love was never about ownership.

It was never about making someone stay—it was about *choosing* them, every single day, even when they had already walked away. And I chose her.

I chose her happiness, her peace, her freedom, even if it meant I had to admire her from afar.

I wanted her to *be*—in whatever way she chose. I wanted her to live fully, to love freely, to chase her dreams without ever feeling tied down. I wanted her to find joy in the little things, to smile without hesitation, to laugh without restraint.

And even if that happiness wasn't found in my arms, even if I was nothing more than a faded memory in her story, I would still find solace in the knowledge that she was *happy.*

I wanted to hear that she was doing well, even if I was no longer the one, she shared her victories with. I wanted to know that life was kind to her, that the world hadn't taken away the light she carried within her.

I wanted to believe that somewhere, she was still the same beautiful soul I once knew—the girl who walked into my life like a quiet miracle and left behind an unshakable love that would live in me forever.

Because love—*real* love—is not about holding on with clenched fists, not about forcing someone to stay, not about begging the universe to rewrite fate. Love is not about possession, about control, about bending someone's will to match your own desires.

Real love is about *letting go* when you have to.

It is about understanding that sometimes, the person you love is meant to walk a path different from yours.

It is about knowing that love is not measured by how tightly you hold on, but by how deeply you can cherish someone even from a distance.

It is about loving without conditions, without expectations, without the need for reciprocation.

And if her presence, even from a distance, was all I was allowed to have, then I would still take it. I would take knowing she was out there, somewhere, laughing, living, becoming the person she was meant to be—even if I was no longer beside her.

I would take the quiet comfort of knowing she was happy, even if I was not the reason behind it. I would take it over a lifetime of meaningless love with anyone else—over forced conversations, over empty embraces, over shallow connections that could never touch the depth of what I felt for her.

No matter how much time passed, no matter how many people entered my life, there was one truth I could never deny:

She was enough. She was always enough.

Her existence alone was enough to make my love worth it, even if she never loved me back in the way I had once wished.

Because love is not about how much you receive—it is about how much you are willing to give, even when there is nothing in return.

And for her, I would always give.

I never wished to call you mine,
To bind your heart, to draw a line.
I never sought to hold you tight,
Just wanted you within my sight.

I never longed to cage your soul,
To write your name on love's control.
I only wished to stand nearby,
To hear your laughter, watch you fly.

Your presence was my quiet peace,
A tender touch, a breath, a crease.
No title, bond, or promised vow,
Just knowing you were here—somehow.

I did not ask for love declared,
For whispered oaths, for hearts laid bare.
I only wished for time and space,
To hold a glimpse of your embrace.

No need for words, no need for chains,
No need to map out love's remains.
I did not beg you not to stray,
I knew you'd leave, yet loved the same way.

I prayed in silence, soft and low,
That fate was kind, yet let you go.
For love was never win or lose,
It wasn't something we could choose.

It lived in moments, pure and bright,
In stolen glances, in borrowed light.
It was the way your name felt right,
The way you lived inside my sight.

Not mine to have, not mine to claim,
Yet still, I loved—without a name.

The Final Realization

Love That Stays, Even When She Doesn't

Love, I have come to understand, is not always about endings. It is not always about the grand reunion, the moment when fate bends in your favor, when the person you long for finally returns.

It is not always about second chances or rewriting the past into a future that should have been.

For the longest time, I waited. I whispered her name into my prayers, hoping that if I said it enough times, the universe would hear me.

I tried to run from the memories, only to find that they had built a home inside me. I tried to chase them, believing that if I could just hold on tight enough, they would lead me back to her.

I searched for her in places she had never been, in people she had never met, in moments she shouldn't have existed in—but somehow, she still did.

She existed in the way certain songs made my heart ache. In the way the air smelled before it rained, reminding me of the way she used to love storms.

In the way my fingers hesitated over my phone, fighting the urge to type out a message I knew would go unanswered.

I told myself that maybe love—*true love*—was about holding on. About not letting go, no matter how much time passed.

But love, I have come to realize, is not just about holding on to a person.

It is also about knowing *what* to hold on to.

I have learned the art of letting go of *her*, while holding on to *us*.

I have let go of the idea that love must always be lived to be real. I have let go of the expectation that love must always lead to togetherness.

I have let go of the need to keep searching for her in a world where she has already chosen her path.

But I have not let go of the memories.

I have not let go of the nights we spent talking about dreams we never got to chase together.

I have not let go of the way she looked at me when she thought I wasn't watching, the way she made the simplest moments feel like magic.

I have not let go of the love itself, because love like this does not demand an ending.

I have learned that letting go does not mean forgetting. That moving forward does not mean erasing the past.

And so, I will carry her with me—not in longing, not in sorrow, but in the quiet, eternal way that love remains—woven into my soul, whispering through time, untouched by distance, unbroken by fate.

Not as a wound.

Not as regret.

But as something beautiful. Something that once was and always will be.

It does not mean forgetting. It does not mean unloving. It does not mean erasing the moments that once made my heart feel alive.

It means understanding that love does not always need to be reciprocated to be real.

That love is not defined by how it ends, but by how deeply it was felt. That some love stories are not meant to reach a destination—they simply *are.*

And sometimes, they exist not to be fulfilled, but to change you, to shape you, to become both the softest and yet the strongest part of who you are.

I am not sure when I finally realized that she was not coming back.

Maybe it was gradual—one unanswered message at a time, one moment of seeing her name and feeling a dull ache instead of unbearable pain.

Or maybe it was all at once, like a wave I had been holding back finally crashing over me, forcing me to admit what I had been running from:

She had moved on.

And I had to move on, too.

But not in the way people expect.

Not by letting go of the love I carried for her. Not by forcing myself to unlove her, to forget the way she made me feel, to pretend that she was just another person passing through my life.

I had to move on from the *idea* of us ever being together again. From the hope that someday, fate would intervene and bring her back.

From the belief that if I just waited long enough, loved deeply enough, the universe would rearrange itself in my favor. But I would never move on from *her*.

I would never move on from the love that had grown inside me, from the memories that lived in my soul.

Because love like this does not fade with time. It does not disappear with distance. It does not vanish just because life decides to take a different path.

She may no longer be in my life. But she will always be a part of me.

And I will carry her—not as a burden, not as a wound, not as something that holds me back—but as something beautiful, something eternal.

Because real love does not need to be lived to be true.

Some love stories exist not to be completed, but simply to *exist.*

I do not move on, I do not forget,
Love like this holds no regret.
Not in her arms, not in her sight,
Yet she still lives in my quiet nights.

Not in my future, not in my past,
Yet in my heart, she'll always last.
I let go of dreams, of what could be,
But not of the love she left in me.

She walks a path I'll never tread,
Yet her name still drifts within my head.
Not as sorrow, not as pain,
But as a love I'd choose again.

Love is not lost, though she is gone,
It echoes, it hums, it still lives on.
Not every love needs a place to arrive,
Some simply exist—to keep us alive.

What Love Has Left Me With

It did not abandon me in the wreckage of what could have been, nor did it strip me of the ability to love again.

Love did not come to destroy me, to hollow me out, or to leave me bitter with what it failed to give. Instead, it left me with something far greater—a depth of feeling I had never known before.

It gave me the ability to love in a way that was pure, undemanding, and limitless.

It taught me that love is not measured by the time it lasts, but by the way it changes you, by the way it shapes the very core of your existence.

I have learned that love is not about keeping someone—it is about experiencing them.

It is about seeing them for everything they are, in all their beauty, in all their imperfections, in all the little details that make them who they are.

It is about appreciating the way their laughter turns an ordinary moment into something golden, about cherishing the way their silences speak louder than any words ever could.

It is about watching them exist—not as someone meant for you, not as someone to be claimed—but simply as themselves.

And even if they leave, even if their path was never meant to intertwine with yours forever, the love you felt for them was never wasted.

Because love, when it is real, does not require an ending to validate its existence.

She may not be my present, and she may not be my future, but she was my transformation.

She was the love that reshaped the way I understood the world, the way I understood myself. The love that turned pain into poetry, longing into lessons, and absence into something that could still be cherished rather than resented.

She was not just a passing moment in time—she was a force that altered my very existence, leaving behind something far more permanent than presence.

She was the love that taught me that not all love stories are meant to be lived forever. Some are meant to be felt so deeply, so profoundly, that they change you at your core.

Some people do not come into your life to stay—they come to shift something inside you, to awaken a part of your soul that you never even knew existed.

She came like a quiet storm, rearranging everything I thought I knew about love. And when she left, she did not take everything with her—she left behind a version of me that was different, deeper, more aware of what it truly meant to love.

She was the kind of love that doesn't just fade into the background of memory. She was the kind of love reflects in the details—the love that echoes in familiar places, in old songs, in moments of stillness where my heart remembers what it once held.

She was the love that taught me that love does not always need to last to be real. That love does not lose its meaning just because it did not reach the ending, I once hoped for.

She was the love that proved that some people, no matter how briefly they stay, leave a mark so deep that no amount of time, no amount of distance, can erase it.

She was that love.

And she always will be.

The love that taught me that sometimes, the greatest love stories are not the ones that end in togetherness, but the ones that change you so profoundly that they become a part of you, written into your soul, long after the person is gone.

The kind of love that does not need forever to be real. The kind of love that does not need reciprocation to have meaning.

The kind of love that, despite never reaching the ending you once prayed for, still feels eternal—because it was never about time, or fate, or what could have been.

It was about feeling something rare, something raw, something that most people spend a lifetime searching for.

And though she may never return, though life may never grant me the reunion I once begged the universe for, the love I had for her will remain.

It will not fade, nor crumble, nor be reduced to nothingness with the passing of time.

It will not remain as regret, because there was nothing to regret in loving her. It was never a mistake, never a burden, never something I wished had never happened.

It will not remain as longing, because love should not be measured by the ache of what was lost, but by the beauty of what was felt.

Instead, it will remain as proof—proof that for one moment in time, I loved with everything I had.

That my heart was capable of something vast, something selfless, something so incredibly pure that even time, even distance, even the harshest of realities could not undo it.

She may not be mine. She may never be mine.

But this love?

This love will always belong to me.

And if not in this life, then in the next.

Perhaps then, the universe will be kinder.

"It did not break me,

it built me.

Not in forever,

but in the way it changed me.

She was never mine to hold,

but always mine to love.

And though she is gone,

the love remains—

silent, endless, whole."

A Love Beyond Time

There are some loves that refuse to be contained within the limits of one lifetime. Loves that are too vast, too deep, too entwined with the very essence of who we are to simply fade away.

Loves that leave an imprint on the soul, not as a wound, but as something eternal—a quiet presence that lingers, waiting for the right moment, the right time, the right world.

Maybe ours was one of those loves.

Maybe we were never meant to be in this life. Maybe the timing was always wrong, the circumstances never quite aligned.

Maybe we were given love but not the space to let it grow, to let it become everything it was meant to be.

But if love like ours was strong enough to exist despite everything, then I have to believe it is strong enough to find its way back.

Maybe in another world, we will meet without the weight of unspoken words and untaken chances. Maybe in another time, your hand will reach for mine, and this time, there will be nothing to pull us apart.

No expectations, no fears, no roads leading away from each other—only love, steady and certain, as if it had been waiting for us all along.

I do not know what the universe holds, what fate has written in the pages beyond this life. But if love is meant to be, if souls recognize each other beyond time, then maybe—just maybe—this is not the end.

Maybe love is not bound by a single lifetime.

Maybe we will meet again.

Maybe we will finally find our way home.

If not this life, then the next,

If not this world, where hearts connect,

Perhaps a place where time stands still,

Where love is fate, not just free will.

If not this touch, then another hand,

Reaching for me in shifting sand.

If not these streets, then other ways,

Where love won't leave, where love will stay.

If not this night, then some far dawn,

Where all we lost is never gone.

Where in your eyes, I won't be past,

But home, but truth, but meant to last.

And so, I love, and so, I wait,

Beyond the pull of time and fate.

If not this life, then the next,

Where love returns, and hearts reflect.

One Last Message

Unsent, But Forever Written in My Heart

If this book ever finds its way to you—if, by some twist of fate, these words make it into your hands—I have only one request.

I do not ask for explanations. I do not ask for answers to the questions I once held in my heart. I do not ask for you to undo the past or to rewrite the present.

I ask only for your presence.

Because your presence—just knowing, you were there—was always enough to bring me peace. It was the calm in the storm, the certainty in the midst of all my uncertainties. You never had to say anything, never had to promise anything—just *being* was enough. The knowledge that you were walking somewhere under the same sky, breathing in the same world, carrying forward in a life I was no longer a part of, was both my greatest comfort and my deepest ache.

Your presence was never about proximity. It was never about needing you beside me, never about holding you in my arms. It was about knowing you *existed,* that you were living, that you were *you*.

And if that was all I was ever allowed to have, I would take it. I would take it over a lifetime of meaningless love with anyone else.

If I could say one last thing to you, it would not be a plea to come back.

I would not ask for you to change your mind.

I would not beg for the universe to undo what has already been written.

I would simply say this: Thank you.

Thank you for showing me what love feels like in its purest, most unselfish form. Thank you for teaching me that love is not about *owning* someone, not about holding them so tightly that they have nowhere else to go, but about *cherishing* them, even if they are no longer yours to keep.

Thank you for being the person who made me understand that love is not about possession, but about *presence.* About the way someone becomes a part of your world so completely that even when they leave, they never truly do. About the way love does not dissolve with distance, does not fade with time, does not require a future to validate its existence.

Love, I have learned, does not always get to stay. But that does not make it any less real.

I hope you are happy. ***Truly.***

I hope life is kind to you in ways that it never was to us. I hope love is gentle with you, soft and endless and fulfilling in ways that mine never could be for you. I hope that when you wake up in the mornings, you feel light, and when you close your eyes at night, your heart is at peace.

I hope the dreams you once whispered to me in the quiet of the night—the ones you held so delicately, the ones you were afraid to speak too loudly, in case the world might take them away—I hope they have found their way to reality.

And if there is ever a moment—just one—where you wonder if you were loved, if you were cherished, if someone in this world held you as their everything, know that the answer is yes.

It was always yes.

It will always be yes.

And if life ever finds a way—if destiny ever decides to rewrite the course we were given, if the universe chooses to be kind just once—then maybe, in another time, in another life, we will meet again.

Maybe in a world where circumstances are not so cruel, where love is not tested by distance, by time, by the weight of choices made too soon or too late. Maybe in a place where we are free from the hesitations, the fears, the doubts that once stood between us. Maybe then, I will reach for you, and this time, you won't have to let go.

Maybe we will meet as strangers who recognize something familiar in each other's eyes, something unspoken, something that is felt even before words are exchanged. Maybe in that life, we will find what we lost in this one, and there will be no questions, no uncertainty—just the quiet understanding that we were always meant to find our way back. But if not—if this was all we were meant to be, if this was the only life where our souls were allowed to cross paths—then I will not mourn what we lost.

I will not carry it as regret.

I will not hold it as sorrow.

Instead, I will carry it as something *beautiful.* As proof that some loves do not need lifetimes to be eternal, that some people can shape you forever, even if they only stay for a while.

I will carry it as an unbreakable truth in my heart.

Something sacred.

Something infinite.

Something that no ending, no separation, no passage of time could ever take away

And for one last time, I want to say this, not with expectation, not with hope, but simply because it is the truest thing I have ever known:

I love you.

Till the very end.

Beyond separations.

Beyond life and death.

Beyond anything this world could ever take away from me.

I love you—not as the world defines,
Not measured in gain, nor bound by signs.
But like the wind that calls your name,
Soft, unseen, yet just the same.

I love you as our first words spoke,
A quiet shift, a fate awoke.
As if the stars had carved our thread,
A bond unspoken, but widely spread

I love you where no words exist,

Where silence hums, where souls persist.

Where presence alone was all I sought,

A love so rare, it can't be bought.

I love you not to claim or bind,

Not to possess, nor make confined.

But just to know you walked this place,

A radiant light, a gift, a grace.

I love you still, though paths have turned,

Though bridges fell, though futures burned.

I love you through the choice you made,

And wished you joy, though mine decayed.

I love you in the nights I wept,

In whispered prayers, in love I kept.

In ghosts of laughter, soft yet true,

In echoes left, in shades of you.

I love you in the streets unknown,

In cafés where I sat alone.

Where every laugh, each stolen glance,

Revived the past in hollow chance.

I love you in the dreams I chased,

In time I lost, in love misplaced.

In faith I gave the stars above,

To prove you were my destined love.

I love you not for days or years,

Not for a vow that time adheres.

But for a world where we had stayed,

Where love was more than plans unmade.

I love you in the tears unshed,
In words unwritten, prayers unread.
In lessons carved upon my skin,
In love that burned, yet stayed within.

I love you not in pain or grief,
Not in regret, nor lost belief.
But in the gift of knowing this—
To love so deep is endless bliss.

I love you past the hands of fate,
Beyond what ifs, beyond too late.
And if this life has drawn its line,
Then in the next, your love is mine.

There, maybe, love will not just be felt—But lived,
complete, and never melt.

Note to the Readers

To those who have walked through these pages with me,

This is not just a story—it is a piece of my soul laid bare. It is the love I once held, the love I still carry, the love that shaped me in ways I never thought possible.

I wrote this not to seek sympathy, not to rewrite fate, and not to hold onto something that has already left my hands.

I wrote this because some loves are too vast to be kept inside a single heart. They need to be shared, to be spoken into existence, to be remembered beyond just one person. I did not write this to dwell on the past or to convince the world that my love was more special than any other.

I wrote it because it was *real.* Because it existed. And because sometimes, that is enough.

Love is not always about happy endings. It is not always about grand reunions, about fate magically intervening to bring two souls back together.

It is not always about the promises that last a lifetime, or the dreams that find their way into reality.

Sometimes, love is about *learning to carry the absence*. About accepting that some stories, no matter how deeply they are felt, are not meant to reach the ending we once imagined.

It is about finding beauty in what *was*, rather than mourning what *could have been*. It is about treasuring the moments we were given, even when they were cut short, even when they ended too soon.

It is about understanding that some people come into our lives not to stay, but to *change us*. And that does not make their love any less real, any less valuable.

We are taught to measure love by longevity, by togetherness, by the certainty of forever. But the truth is, love does not need to last a lifetime to be *infinite*.

Some love stories exist in transient moments, in stolen glances, in the unspoken words that live between two people who once meant everything to each other

Some love stories are written in the quiet, in the spaces between what was said and what was left unsaid.

And I want you to know this—love, in its *purest* form, does not need reciprocation to be meaningful.

It does not need a destination to be eternal. It does not need a name, a label, or a promise to be *real*.

Love is not defined by how it ends, but by how deeply it was felt.

Love is in the way someone changes you, in the way they shape your world, in the way they leave an imprint so deep that no amount of time, no amount of distance, no amount of moving forward can erase it.

Because love, when it is true, does not simply disappear. It dwells. It stays. It becomes a part of who you are. And sometimes, that is enough.

So, if you have ever loved someone who could never be yours, if you have ever stayed awake at night whispering silent prayers to the universe, hoping for just one more moment, one more chance, one more rewrite of fate—then know this: you are not alone.

If you have ever carried a name inside your heart, a love that no one else understood, a longing that was never spoken aloud, then understand that love like that does not make you weak.

It does not make you foolish. It does not mean you failed.

It simply means you *felt*—deeply, selflessly, wholly. And that is something beautiful.

Know that love, even if it does not stay, even if it does not end the way you once dreamed, is *never wasted*.

Love is not measured by the length of time it lasts, nor by the way it concludes, but by the way it changes you.

By the way it shapes you, the way it opens your heart, the way it teaches you what it means to truly care for someone beyond the boundaries of expectation.

I have learned that love is not about *holding on to a person*—because sometimes, no matter how much you love them, no matter how deeply you wish they would stay, life has a different plan.

But love is about holding on to the *feeling*.

I have learned to let go of the idea of being with her, to accept that she was never meant to be a part of my future.

But I will never let go of the love I had for her. Because that love was real. That love made me who I am.

That love will always live within me, not as regret, not as sorrow, but as proof that I once loved with everything I had.

And if you take anything from this story, if these words leave any imprint on your heart,

let it be this:

Love fully. Love without fear, without hesitation, without wondering if it will last. Love for the sake of loving, even when there are no guarantees, even when you know it might not be returned in the way you hope.

Love fearlessly. Love even when it is uncertain, even when it is desiccating, even when it hurts. Because to love, even in the face of loss, even in the face of impossibility, is to be *alive*.

And love—real, pure, selfless love—is always worth it. And if not in this life, then in the next, maybe love will find its way back home.

With all that I have,

With all that I was,

And with all that I will always be, ***I loved.***

This book is not just a story—it is a piece of my heart, a collection of emotions that I have lived through, loved through, and lost through. But as much as this is an ending, I still hold onto the quiet hope that life is not done writing our story.

If fate is ever kind enough to bring her back to me—if I ever get the chance to live the love I have prayed for, to rewrite the chapters we never got to finish—then I will write another part.

Not from a place of longing, but from a place of love finally realized. Until that day comes, these words will remain as they are—a tribute to a love that, even in its incompleteness, shaped me in ways nothing else ever could.

Note to the Readers

www.ingramcontent.com/pod-product-compliance
Lightning Source LLC
LaVergne TN
LVHW091323150826
845673LV00006B/1742